POETRY AND HAIKU-STYLE VERSE

MOSTLY

INSPIRED BY NATURE

POETRY AND HAIKU-STYLE VERSE

MOSTLY

INSPIRED BY NATURE

Catherine Morton

Edited by Daniel Duff

Poetry and Haiku-Style Verse Mostly Inspired by Nature

By Catherine E. Morton

Edited by Daniel G. Duff

ISBN: 9798636171379

Independently published

Printed in the United States of America.

To my husband

Contents

The Rhine

Majestic, powerful but gentle too
It flows perpetually towards the sea
winding, turning, lapping at the shoreline
foaming on the grey pebbles
on the white sea-shelled sand.

A Heron stands sentinel and barks
to another on the other side.
As laden barges ply their trade
with coal, tractors and the like

The water flows under myriad bridges
while on the top people are looking
down at the massive breadth of water
speeding past. In the baylets
families having picnics
paddle, play and splash!

On summer nights crickets chirp intensely

The full moon lights up the bridges

and the factory too,

while lovers walk hand in hand

Towards orange sunsets

Which melt into the darkness

But still she flows.

In the daytime gulls wheel above the water,

when choppy, bob like corks noisily calling

Egyptian Geese sit and stand around

while swans dabble in the waterweeded
edges.

In summer flowers bloom on the riverbank

chives, yellow bedstraw, large speedwell
and woad,

while insects thrive and add their noise to
the cacophony.

So grandly it flows its course

~~winding, turning, lapping at the shoreline~~

music, literature and art, all inspired by
this Goliath.

A young lad throws pebbles

which skims across 5 times, then 3

A Kingfisher called, just flew across,

halcyon blue flash, leaving wonderment on

a woman's face.

Majestic, powerful, but gentle too

the Rhine flows perpetually towards the sea

winding, turning, lapping at the shoreline.

foaming on the grey pebbles

on the white, sea-shelled sand.

The Jewel in the Sand

We stand transfixed

For on the path we see

magnificence, resplendent

In the colours of imperial robes

glistening in the hazy sunlight

glorious purples and golds

A creature shimmering with scintillating
blue

as it shuffles slowly on the soiled sand

probing and sifting with its yellow
proboscis

like an elephant's trunk, carefully caressing
the ground

searching for moisture and minerals,

so delicately it bends.

But in an instant, like a mirage it vanishes

And in its place a dusky dark-winged
creature sits

Then just as unexpectedly the iridescence returns

Ephemeral velvet riches reappear

As the sunlight catches its scales again

firing the spectacle, like breath to the embers of a dying fire

We feel privileged to witness this creature

And to have watched its behaviour so intimately

We notice it has lost an orange eye-spot

whilst one wing bears an open tear

Battle scars that tell of a near-death experience

with a bird, a hungry shrike perhaps

So long have I yearned to see one such as this

But never imagined how beautiful it would be

So unexpectedly we came across it,

like a jewel in the sand,

my first ever Purple Emperor!

Will I live to see the morning?

Will I live to see the morning?

Will the light conquer the dark

and let the morning rays of sunlight

shine on my face as I lie in bed?

Will I hear my mother's voice?

The sweetest voice that nurtured me
through life,

which is tempered by the pain of living

but will always be sweet.

Will I hear her tomorrow just the same?

Will I hear my dearest husband?

Will he be pleased to hear me

and give me joy just to hear him speak?

Will I live to see the morning?

Will the light conquer the dark

and let the morning rays of sunlight

shine on my face as I lie in bed?

Will I speak to my dear friend, Janet?

Always interesting and a bright spark

Also Sue, kind and welcoming

Both warriors of life

Aren't we all warriors?

Will I hear the birdsong when I awake?

Sparrows chirping and melodious blackbirds

Bird song that lifts my heart

Will I hear Tweet of the Day?

The interesting world topics of Today?

Will there be happiness and kindness

as well as pain?

Will I live to see the morning?

Will the light conquer the dark

and let the morning rays of sunlight

shine on my face as I lie in bed?

Will I open my eyes to a bright new day?

Amaryllis

Open one by one

Trumpet flowers of crimson

Cheer the winter gloom

Fire Salamander

Rainy autumn night

Fire Salamander posing

Black yellow and bright

Alexandrine Parakeets

Noisy green parrots

Winter acrobatic fun

Trees laden with nuts

Magnolia Tree

Large flower lanterns

Glorious on leafless tree

White pink springtime joy

Mistle Thrushes

Midday in tree tops

Strong spotted thrush feasts on fruit

Smears seed on branches

Cranes Migrating

Bird Squadrons calling

Spring and autumn migrations

Fly past not stopping

"Grus" out of the blue

Is it? Can it really be?

Bugling cranes go through

Firecrest

Zip zip zip Flutter

Orange crest, white eye stripe flash

Hiss hiss happy trill

Winter Birding

Wintry lakeside scene

Distant diving ducks feeding

Bitter cold birding

Köln (Cologne) Park

Young geese in winter
Handy for hungry Goshawks
One by one they´re gone

Red-Backed Shrike

Prey skewered on thorns
Sharp eyes, hooked beak, pinky breast
Swoops down on lizard

Tawny Owl

Busy road by wood

On a pole a twinkling eye

Day roost for Ta Woo!

Eagle Owl

Huge wings, orange eyes

Silent night flyer U-Hoo

Fear maker, Top Dog!

Robin

A gardener's friend

In spring vying for females

Red breast fights red breast

Long-tailed Tit

Winter band of tits

Long-tailed they make a trill call

Cold night, it's a ball!

Day Break

Day break Reddened sky

Greylag Geese fly honking by

Two sitting cows moo

Gannets

Sea bird right angled

Catching the spray, black white soars

Dives in winter seas

Heron

Wing shading still pool

Eyes transfixed in evening light

Spears a silver fish

Nuthatch

Day-time upside down

Bird hops down the trunk calling

Flies up to descend

Grasshoppers

Noon flash, blue flash, jump
Disappears in sand and dirt
Camouflage magic!

Goldcrest

Yellow stripe on crown
Flitting with comical face
Flies down up away!

Magpies

Robber birds gather

Black white corvids with long tail

Noisy chattering

Black Redstart

Dusky with red tail

Roof top tiles its preference

Or else on a fence!

Male Redstart

Red tail shimmering

Black mask with striking white blaze

A late spring migrant

Bats

Darkness envelopes

Twilight bats circle the lake

Swooping on their prey

Firefly

Glow fade and glow bright!
Try to catch it, nothing there
Spiders trap light on!

Kestrel

Chestnut, braced, kite-like
Hovers against a blue sky
Summer's mouse hunter!

Starling

Iridescent black

Evening murmuration

Intoxicating!

Hedgehogs

Prickly ball when scared

Feeding on insects and worms

Good swimmer, rare now

Badgers

Striped face rolling gait

Powerful paws prise tulips

Nocturnal wormer

Wood Pigeons

Black Ivy berries

Pigeons upside down feeding

Dextrous parrot like!

Jumping Spider

Small, jumper, no web

Pounce, its style of catching prey

Fun to watch it jump

Grass Snake

One June it slithered

Swam in water whiplash-like

Surprising a frog!

Green Hairstreak

Tiny butterfly

In the midday sun it gleams

Iridescent green!

Buzzard

Large wings in blue sky

Bird swoops down for a rabbit

Then crows drive it off!

Red Squirrel

Agile tree climber

Russet fur and bushy tail

Winter nut planter!

Ring-Ouzel

Autumn sightings rare

Blackbird, white bib, shy hopper

They're Morocco bound!

Swallows

Harbingers of spring

Fork-tailed twitterers catch flies

Sweep down across fields

Turtle Dove

Beautiful purring

On a branch, throat vibrating

A dove now quite rare!

Lily-of-the-valley

Sweet smell wafts through trees

White waxy flowers unfurl

German woods in May!

Pear Tree

Majestic Pear Tree

Bedecked in white spring blossom

Hides a wild bee nest

Sparrows

Forsythia Bush

Sparrows greet me each morning

With their chirpy song!

Bullace Hedge

Glorious blossom

White spring spires perfume the air

Pulsating bird song

Green Woodpeckers

Birds hopping on lawns

Yaffle call, green anteaters

Tree holes for a nest!

Fox

With its jaunty gait

Red brown fur and pointy ears

It crosses the field!

Brimstone

Sulphur butterfly
Fluttering fast, first of year
March-time spirit lift

Notre Dame

Ancient Cathedral
Tragic fire, it lost its spire
Then resurrected?

Wild boar Piglets

Midday piglets doze

Stripy bodies, curly tails

Waiting for moon rise

Swallows Return

Today joyfulness

The swallows are here again

I can hear their joy!

May Fly

They rise up from streams
Fly for one brief day, they mate
Then sadly they die!

Gulls

Feeding the angels
Family photos with white gulls
Hanging in sunlight

White Cliffs of Dover

Walking the white cliffs

Early Spider Orchid there

Stunning scenery

Fieldfares

Fieldfares at twilight

Display, chattering, slow flight

Up to a tree top

Glow Worm

Summer nights it glows

A stationary lantern

Drawing in the males

Wahner Heide Heath

Yellow blaze in spring

Glorious broom flowering

Coconut scented

Military Orchids

Rare pink flower spikes

Helmeted with hair buttons

Spring Eifel jewels

Swifts

Swifts scream circling round

Rakish masters of the sky

Sleep high on the wing

Eifel

Hills, streams and black storks
Wild cats roam, rare orchids flower
Spring brings Red Kites back

Bee Eaters

Surprise! Pree pree calls
15 Bee Eaters flew past
They're on migration

Blackcap

Loud fluty songster

Smart black cap gives it its name

Maytime serenade

Blackbird

Black-bird, yellow bill

Almost a nightingale song

Twilight winter charm

Nightingale

Loud, beautiful song

Night and day from a large bush

To pull a female

Schloss Benrath Stately Home

Rococo treasure

Lakeside palace reflections

Pink-white in sunlight

Cherry Blossom

Cherry blossom spring

Pink or white translucent blooms

Scented branches hum

About the author:

Catherine Morton was brought up on a farm near Huntingdon, Cambridgeshire, in the UK. She was one of six children and has always had a love of nature and many interests. She has spent time in Germany as well as England, and has been inspired by nature in both countries.

Printed in Poland
by Amazon Fulfillment
Poland Sp. z o.o., Wrocław

56693322R00031